© 1977 Almark Publishing Co. Ltd.

Text & Illustations ©
Roy Dilley & Bryan Fosten

All rights reserved. No part of this publication may be reproduced, stored in a retrieval system or transmitted by any means electronic, mechanical, or by photo-copying, without prior permission of the publishers.

First Published 1977.

ISBN 0 85524 293 0

Printed in Great Britain by
Staples Printers Ltd.,
Trafalgar Road, Kettering,
Northamptonshire,
for the publishers, Almark Publishing Co. Ltd.
49 Malden Way, New Malden,
Surrey KT3 6EA, England.

No. 3 DIORAMAS & SCENIC SETTINGS

By
Roy Dilley & Bryan Fosten

*Almark Publishing Co. Ltd.,
London*

INTRODUCTION

The use of scenic backgrounds and settings, against or in which models can be displayed has become an accepted means by which added realism, and hence effectiveness can be conveyed. The practice has been a feature of railway modelling for many years, but it is really only over the past decade or so that it has been at all widespread among enthusiasts for military miniatures. Scenery used for war-gaming tends to be of a formalized nature and is not part of the subject matter of this present volume. Of course, the very nature of 'toy' soldiers, produced commercially as single figures each on its own integral stand, encouraged individual display or mass effects with a minimum of simple scenery, the stands being awkward to hide or disguise in more elaborate or realistic groundwork. It must also be admitted that the figures themselves tended to be produced in stiff 'parade-ground' attitudes, whilst commercial painting and indeed the 're-painting' of earlier amateurs, was for the most part done in shiny enamel finishes, unsuitable for conveying any strong sense of reality. The wonder is that such basic attempts as were made came off as well as they did; but only few attempts at effective scenic work in military modelling were made before World War Two, although strikingly competent results had been achieved by Capt. Siborne in his two great representations of the Battle of Waterloo, constructed as early as the middle of the nineteenth century.

Improvements in manufacturing processes, the advent of 'connoisseur' figures, and the development of 'conversion', 'scratch-building', and painting techniques have meant that military modellers in the years since 1945, have become more and more capable of producing pieces which depict their prototypes with great fidelity, and which gain even more conviction from being placed in a setting representative of real life. Many vehicles, guns equipment and accessories of all kinds are now available as kits or ready made items, and a great variety of 'scenic' materials can be obtained to assist in the production of settings. Add to these all those 'natural' and domestic items that a modeller's imagination can press into service, and it will be seen that the possibilities for achieving realism in backgrounds and settings for models are almost unlimited.

However, lest the newcomer to military modelling should become carried away by the wealth of material at his disposal, and be led into believing that only numbers in elaborate settings are what should be aimed at, let the point be made that a single figure, nicely painted and with a modicum of groundwork imaginatively applied, can be as effective in its way as a grand battle-scene. Ideally, (whether intended as a representation of an actual historical event, or as a purely imaginative composition), the setting should combine with the model to establish a situation, or 'tell a story', and it is this narrative quality which seizes the imagination of the observer and leads him to 'see' the piece in a realistic and hence convincing light. It is widely accepted nowadays that military modelling is an art form and the creations resulting from its practice are true 'objects d'art', for just as the pictorial artist convinces the beholder by means of marks and colours applied to a flat surface that he sees real forms and distances, so the modeller creates with his scraps of metal and plastic a 3-dimensional 'picture' with the same objective. The principles of composition apply to a diorama or setting equally as to a picture, whilst competent use of colour and contrast is important to both forms of representation. Clearly dioramas and scenic settings, cover the whole gamut of displaying military miniatures, from the embellishment of a single piece, via small and large groups of models, to the depiction of a complete battle scene or ceremonial parade. However it is important to stress that, whilst the setting should not overpower the main subject or subjects of the composition, neither should it be of so crude or perfunctory a nature as to detract from the impression created by the piece as a whole. A logical approach will make it plain that settings need as much research and attention to detail as the principal subjects themselves, so that the environments represented avoid inconsistency or absurdity. Even in a small setting, the background must be believable in all its facets, or the impact of a well-designed model will be considerably lessened, even completely destroyed. Yet, given imagination in concept and skill in execution, extremely convincing situations can be set up in surprisingly small areas. The question of overall size is important, especially where space available for display is restricted, and will often be a significant factor in taking a decision about the choice and presentation of a subject. Always to be kept in mind is the impression it is desired that the finished piece shall convey, and how best it may be achieved with the models, materials, display space and techniques that are available. Plus, of course, imagination, for it is on the exercise of this attribute in the creation of original work that the modeller will, in the end, rely for success.

Truly the subject range for military modelling is enormous, taking in the whole sweep of life under arms, from the earliest times to the present. Training, routine, recreational and domestic incidents, with the day to day aspects of campaigning in and out of combat, provide almost inexhaustible scope for modelling subjects, and it must not be forgotten, the military life exists alongside that of the civilian touching and intermingling with it on frequent occasions, some hum-drum, some tragic, others humourous or light-hearted. Soldiers have chosen, or been thrust into a particular way of life; dioramas and settings help the military modeller to depict any of the multitudinous aspects and incidents of that life in a conveniently packaged way.

Obviously, a project carelessly carried out will rarely produce the desired result; flair and economy are not the same as haste and slap dash work, so the modeller who is serious in his regard for his hobby will want to spare no effort in learning and improving the skills and techniques that will enable him to make the most of his abilities. In this book are suggested some ways in which dioramas and settings can be constructed to give effectively convincing results. It is up to you, the reader, to utilise your imagination and flair in adopting and adapting these suggestions in the development of your own unique creations.

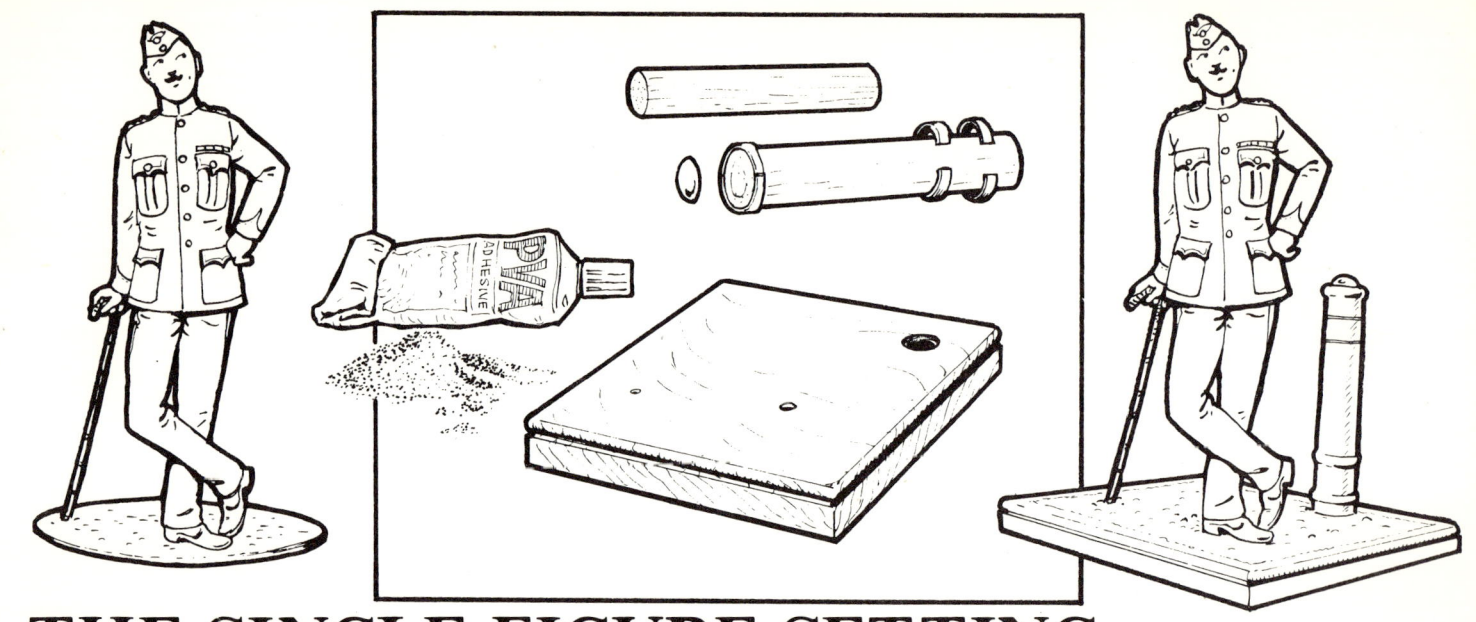

THE SINGLE FIGURE SETTING

Because of its isolated circumstance the single model needs particular care when a choice is being made in respect of pose and location so that incongruity or absurdity can be minimised. Situations in which the subject seems to be in the position of reacting directly with some other, non-represented, are difficult to handle convincingly, and should therefore be avoided unless the modeller is sure of the effect he wishes to create. Violent action may also present serious problems when depicted by a single model, which can very easily, become bizarre, like a child playing at being King Arthur, and slashing wildly around himself at invisible enemies. On the other hand, more sedate or self contained actions and activities can be represented very successfully by single figures, often becoming more compelling by the concentration of the observer's interest, and whereas formerly the individual piece on a plain plinth looked perhaps somewhat isolated and artificial, the gradual change to decoration of the base and its transition to a small environment makes such a single presentation today much more natural.

Whilst for reasons of good composition a single figure setting will not usually be very large in relation to its subject, it can be made quite definitely into a 'place' as opposed to just a 'base', and reference to some of the accompanying photographic examples will make this point very forcibly.

A useful formula for use when choosing a subject, and particularly suitable to the single-figure, is the one known as the "Five W's" Who? What? Where? When? and Why? By applying this formula it is possible to visualise the finished model in all its essential particulars before a single step has been made in the actual modelling. This means that ideas are crystallized into firm working 'blue-prints' without the costly wastage of time and materials that can occur with trial and error type projects. In greater detail, the headings cover:

WHO? Is the figure to represent an actual personality? If not, try to be specific about the identity of its prototype, e.g. Grenadier Officer of the 28th Regiment. WHAT? What is the figure to be doing and how is it armed and equipped? WHERE? Consideration can be both general e.g. France, Belgium, Waterloo, Lucknow, and specific, e.g. behind a ruined wall, crossing a field, etc. WHEN? This covers the actual or approximate period, e.g. June 18th 1815, 4 pm., summer 1857; and the circumstances of the time, e.g. during the lull in the battle, at evening orders. Time of day may be important in specific cases. WHY? Here the reason for the action or location of the figure is examined, e.g. steadying the line, preparing to advance, etc.

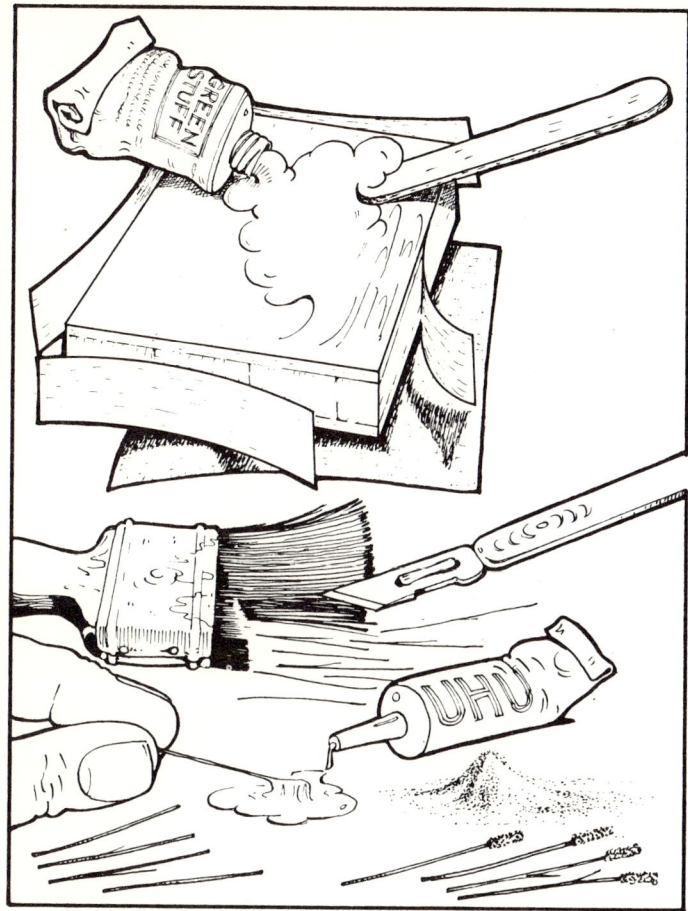

With practice, the image of the proposed figure that becomes established in the minds'-eye by using the formula, will be found to be surprisingly detailed, and attitude, dress and setting will practically suggest themselves.

SINGLE FIGURES

Bearing in mind the principles of good composition, and application of the 'Five W's' formula, it is now possible to consider the actual creation of a single figure in its setting. The example given is an actual piece, produced by a novice, which won an important national competition.

The subject is a soldier of the 23rd Regt. during the afternoon of June 18th 1815, standing in the wet and trampled corn on the slope above the Chateau of Hougoumont awaiting yet another onrush by the French, and it will be seen that this description covers all aspects of the 'Five W's'. Assembled from a Stadden designed figure issued some years or so ago by Almark, the subject stands in the 'on guard' position, with bayonet fixed, and, before painting, was used to assist with the composition of the setting. This was kept simple, consisting of a square of blockboard faced with oak veneer and with a piece of baize glued to its underside. A textured surface was made from a thin application of Green Putty to represent the earth of the field, into which a number of corn-stalks were inserted, these being made from bristles cut from an old paste-brush, dipped into glue at one end and sprinkled with sand to make the 'ears'. The Green Putty was painted in earth colour, then varnished to give the wet effect, and the 'corn' was finished in shades of green, it was not yet ripe remember, and the stalks disordered as if somewhat trampled. After careful painting the figure was pegged into the surface, in the position decided upon earlier, and the piece was labelled with Dymo-type as a finishing touch.

In this way a straightforward model was given character and purpose, simply yet most effectively.

Our Second example in this section is a little more elaborate, yet succeeds in its purpose without fussiness or overcrowding. The figure represents a French Staff Officer of the Napoleonic period stretched out on the ground taking a hard-earned nap, his head resting comfortably against a boulder, and his sword, stuck into the ground at his side, ready for action in the event of sudden necessity. Exquisitely put together as a 'conversion' from Historex basic parts, the figure is excellently proportioned and conveys an authentically relaxed appearance, with the painting carried out in a most accomplished fashion. The same care has been shown in the construction of the base and scenic details, the simulated grass, and the boulder being exactly right. Again, a single figure has been given an unusual and completely successful realistic treatment, fitting most convincingly into its environment only an inch or so square.

In neither of our examples have the modellers been guilty of over-elaboration: the subjects are simply posed in static positions against just sufficient groundwork to create the impression of a 'real' location. Neat finishes to the actual bases complete both pieces, differing in style and content, yet eminently successful in their treatment.

Among the photographs accompanying this section will be found other instances of the use of single figures in settings which help to establish an air of reality.

SIMPLE GROUPS

A group for the purposes of modelling, may be defined as, 'Two or more human figures which form a complete design'. This uncomplicated definition allows for reaction of figures one with another and for the addition of animals, guns and any other sort of equipment or accessories relevant to a 'situation' and location. Simple groups, with two or three figures and their supporting items in a setting, are very popular, can be extremely effective in creating atmosphere and narrative 'punch', and being generally of manageable size, create a minimum of storage and display problems.

This type of presentation, which may be further described as 'mini-diorama', 'vignette' or 'conversation piece', is particularly suitable for the expression of a single idea, boldly stated, and with just sufficient in the way of setting to establish the sense of location without undue clutter. It truly becomes a matter of good composition the nice placement of figures and accessories to create the best effect, and careful planning of the piece becomes a matter of some importance.

Having chosen a subject and assembled the reference data, uniform details background items and so on, it is useful to make a few preliminary sketches to establish the figure poses that will best express the theme and the most effective placement of any scenic accessories that may be involved. Book illustrations, photographs and prints often provide the inspiration for groups, and to a certain extent determine figure attitudes and scenic detail, but it is always of value to rough-out the planned group since what comes over with effect in a picture may need amendment in a three-dimensional presentation which may be viewed from many different angles.

Sometimes it is of great advantage to focus the observer's attention upon a prominent scenic or architectural detail, such as an ornamental fountain, a horsetrough, pump, stile, signpost or any other relevant feature, and allow the figures as it were, to fall into position around the focus point in as 'natural' a way as possible. Such groupings can encompass the formal 'drill' attitudes; for example, sentries being changed before a sentry-box, with a length of railing or wall in the background: the relaxed easy postures; such as two or three men around a cooking-fire, with camp accessories about them: and the 'action' or 'combat' positions; i.e. a machine-gun team firing from behind a hedge or bank, or the classic 'man to man' confrontation.

Whatever subject is decided upon, don't pack too much into the simple group, but keep as far as possible to the expression of a single idea.

The chief function of composition is to place the subject before the observer so that his attention is held by it and not distracted by some unimportant point. Its secondary function is to make a pattern pleasing to the eye.

In this first example of a simple group of figures, the object is to show infantry clothing and equipment as it was worn in a particular campaign, the Sudan War of 1884/5, and the subject is a trio of soldiers, an outlying piquet perhaps, firing upon a distant enemy. To avoid monotony of appearance all three men are in different attitudes, directing fire, actually shooting, and reloading, and are so arranged as to encourage the eye of the observer to pass naturally from one figure to the rest without distraction. Groundwork is kept to a minimum both in accord with the desert locale and to allow concentration on the subject, and the whole piece is contained in an area of less than 10 square inches, in fact a moulded plastic base of Historex manufacture.

The figures are conversions of Japanese World War II types in hard plastic, the heads of which were replaced with metal castings depicting the early pattern Wolsely helmet, and the equipment and weapons altered to the correct British pattern for the period.

To simulate the desert environment, coarse sand was sprinkled over a thick coating of 'white' PVA glue on the top surface of the base, some rock fragments were fixed in position, and several scraps of dried out lichen were also added to represent camelthorn. When painted, the figures were secured to the base in the pattern previously determined by a sketch or so, and the composition was complete – simple, but it is felt, effective.

More complex groundwork forms the setting for our second example in this classification, which shows German soldiers of the 1940 period in the ruins of an urban building. The figures form a single subject, an anti-tank rifle team, with commander, gunner and No 2; the weapon itself and the ammunition container box. They were assembled with slight conversion and detailing from a standard kit of parts, and painted in the colours appropriate to the uniforms of the period.

It was neither necessary nor desirable to use a complete ruined building as a setting in view of the small number of figures and the requirements of composition, but some impression of devastation needed to be conveyed.

Several sketches were made to try to establish a suitable grouping of figures and sense of location, and it was decided to depict a fragment of the angle where two walls meet, to include the vestiges of a window opening, and to show traces of woodwork, floors and beams etc, all in a surrounding area of rubble and dust. On the top surface of a piece of blockboard ¾ in. thick and 5 ins. square was spread a liberal coating of PVA glue, over which, at the edges was sprinkled coarse sand. The wall angle (in this case a plastic moulding, but equally well represented by balsa wood shapes coated in plaster or putty with brick or stone courses scribed into it), was then fixed firmly into position, and a heap of rubble was gradually built up around it, using cat-litter, (tiny pieces of decomposed granite, real stone, or brick smashed and broken down would be just as effective). Into the rubble, beams and boards, made from match sticks and short lengths of veneer, were inserted and secured to serve as the damaged woodwork of the building, and matchstick 'frames' were fitted to the window opening. When appropriately painted, 'grimed' and 'smoke-blackened' the setting provided a striking location for the figure models. Varnished veneer edges and a baize underside finished off the base in a tidy and attractive way.

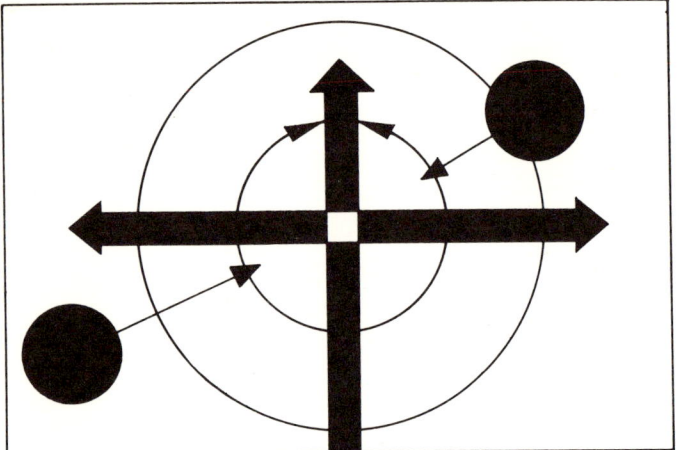

LARGER GROUPS

Groups of more than 3 or 4 figures, and where appropriate, vehicles or other equipment, enable a modeller to enlarge the scope of his presentation and to deal, should he wish to do so, with more than one idea at a time. However, it is all too easy for clutter and over-abundance of background detail to overwhelm the subject(s), and therefore the application of sound composition to the larger group is of the utmost importance in order to make the subject prominent and the presentation pleasing to the observer, thus satisfying both explanatory and aesthetic requirements.

The following may be said to be those principles of composition applicable to good diorama work:

(1). *Simplicity*. Keep the presentation straightforward, with a clear-cut theme.
(2). *Symmetry*. Balance the work so as to reduce those areas of 'no interest' where nothing is happening.
(3). *Proportion*. Ensure that the overall size of the piece is in keeping with the subject(s), and that the setting does not assume undue physical prominence.
(4). *Unity*. The component parts of the presentation should relate one to another and be viewable as a whole.
(5). *Order*. Have a planned approach and avoid clutter.
(6). *Gradation*. This implies that the components should have a logical placement and tonal quality, so that the eye moves easily in steps from one part to the next.
(7). *Subordination*. Where more than one idea is involved, give greater emphasis to the more important.
(8). *Contrast*. Use one figure or feature against another to spotlight differences of action, dress, colour, etc.
(9). *Variety*. Vary the poses and activities of figures to maintain the interest of the spectator. Do the same with aspects of the setting, but do not let it swamp the subject(s).
(10). *Volume*. Try to convey a sense of space, mass and area which is occupied. This does not mean cramming in as much as possible, but rather the careful placement of items in relation to the setting.
(11). *Restraint*. Be moderate and recognise the limits of a model presentation, avoiding overstatement and bludgeoning of the eye with masses of detail and sheer numbers of figures.

In the introduction to this work, the function of these principles has already been stated. Their application to a project, in whole or in part, makes the difference between a striking, good-to-look-at show piece, and a haphazard jumble of ideas, confusing to the eye and lacking ability to convey any coherent theme.

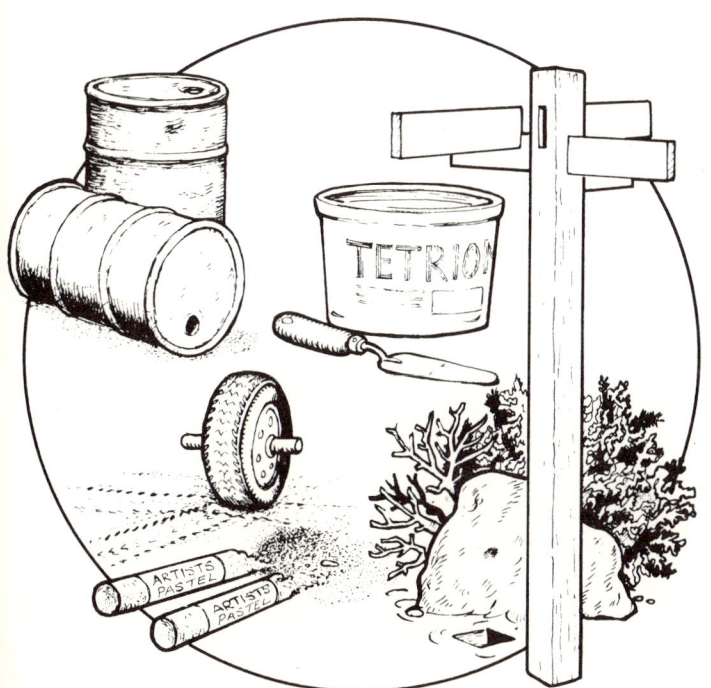

A setting in which figures, a vehicle and various 'natural', manufactured and 'scratch built' scenic items combine, is the subject of our first example in this category. Titled 'Near Kalemyo, 1944', it depicts a military-police traffic controller at the junction of tracks in Burma; the signpost with its several legends really existed.

The base is a 7 ins. square of ½ in. board. Over one surface, previously scored to provide a key, was spread a thin coating of 'Das' modelling clay, impressed with ruts and tyre-marks, and painted in dark earth shades after these had set hard. An irregular diamond of grass matting was glued in one corner, and into this was fixed a quantity of dried sphagnum moss to form the thicket of tropical underbrush. The sign-post was made from Plastruct square section extrusion, with arms of plastic strip. Scale oil-drums from a Tamiya kit of accessories were painted and positioned at the point of the diamond to complete the scenic detail.

The underside of the base was covered with a sheet of green baize, and the edges with strips of wood veneer, these last being given a coat of varnish. Then the painted models were fixed on with PVA glue, the standing figure being pegged additionally into the surface before the whole piece was dusted liberally with powdered artists' pastels.

Soldiers in a more sportive mood feature in our second example in this section. Some French troops of the Napoleonic period are depicted having a little fun at the expense of a scarecrow, whilst a horse stands patiently by and the liquor flows free! The composition conveys a pleasant, lighthearted impression, is nicely balanced and competently executed.

In this case the baseboard chosen has been bevelled at the edges for a more decorative effect, and the groundwork is built up with Plasticine, textured and coloured, and with the raw edges painted black.

Among the accessory details, the scarecrow is a good example of a scratch-built item. On a dowel framework are affixed two hanks of rafia-straw in the shape of a cross, the ends of the horizontal arms being frayed then fitted with 'gloves', these being hands cut from spare plastic arms from the scrap-box. The head is a ball of rafia wrapped in a scrap of linen, tied at the neck and fixed to the top of the upright dowel. After painting, the scarecrow was given a battered cocked-hat, another plastic item from the spares box.

Various wine and liquor bottles litter the scene, and our sketches show how these can be fashioned from pieces of wood or plastic rod. Several manufacturers of scale accessories do however issue packs containing miniature bottles of different shapes and sizes.

ANCILLARY ARTICLES AND ACCESSORIES

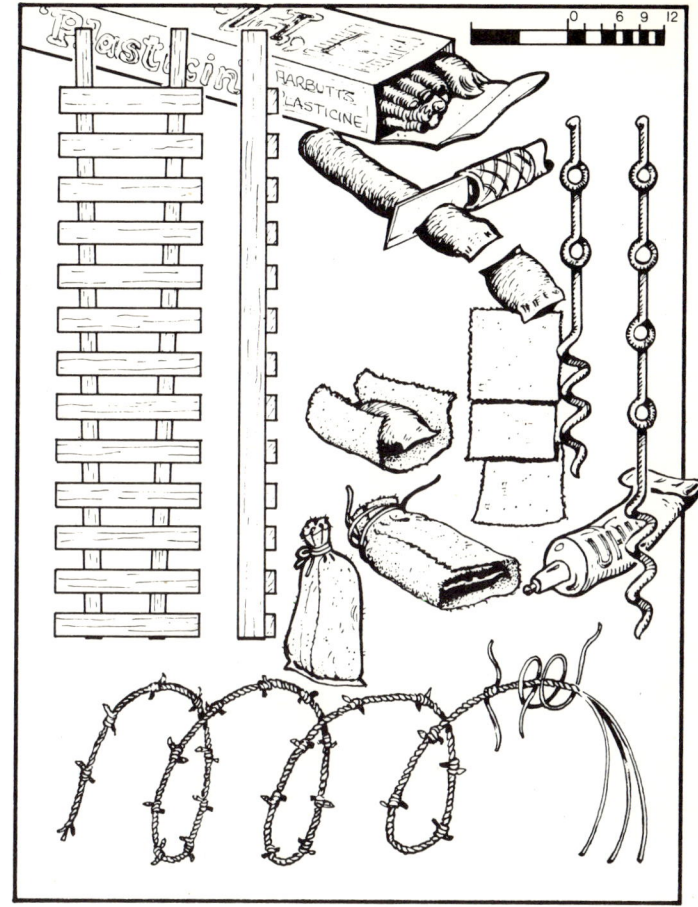

Apart from the actual ground, vegetation and architecture found in an environment, there are frequently items of utility or decoration which contribute to the situation; these would include tools, furniture, various containers, lighting-columns, telegraph-poles, etc., the list is endless. In combat there will probably be quantities of field-engineering stores, ammunition and fuel containers, and some of the myriad equipment details that surround troops on campaign.

Some typical examples of such battlefield impedimenta and how to model them are sketched, and illustrated here in photographs. To produce miniature sandbags in quantity, wrap strips of Plasticine in scrap cloth, linen is ideal, seal the overlap with fabric glue, then cut off the requisite lengths for the bags, securing the cut edges with glue. Trench or 'duck' boards are easily fabricated with strip-wood and veneer, and for barbed-wire twist fine gauge fuze-wire, tie on barbs at intervals, then coil or string it between matchstick or paper-clip 'pickets'. Paper, cloth, card, wood and wire scraps can be utilized for all kinds of detail. Additionally, extensive ranges of scale furniture and equipment are manufactured ready assembled or in kit form by many firms, including Historex, Phoenix, Tamiya and Armour Accessories.

This shows a Gardner-gun detachment of the Royal Navy operating in support of a column in the 1884/5 campaign, with the men grouped around the weapon in action poses, and, directing the fire, an officer with pistol and sword. As a composition, the group is compact and self-contained, with an interesting variety of lively attitudes. Drama is heightened by the austerity of the setting, a flat gravel plain, dotted with rocks and clumps of camel-thorn. Spread thickly over PVA glue, coarse sand, into which fragments of shale and sprigs of dried lichen were impressed, made up the ground surface. Providing the firm base is a rectangle of ¾" thick blockboard, faced with varnished veneer, and covered on the underside with baize.

In this narrative piece, the locale remains the same, but the groundwork has been constructed to allow the figures to be presented at different levels. Entitled 'The Birds have Flown', the diorama depicts a patrol of British soldiers who have found an enemy camp from which the occupants have recently fled, leaving a still smoking fire and a broken, discarded spear. Into the 'standard' desert surface mix of sand, rock-fragments and lichen, has been introduced a large piece of shale, whose conformation supplies a ledge, upon which a figure is posed, and whose various facets reveal differing textures and colouring. Several small chippings have been arranged to make a circular fire-place, in which some lichen twigs smoulder over fluorescent paint embers, with a wisp of cotton-wool teased out to provide a realistic tendril of smoke. The spear is scratchbuilt from plastic sheet and rod.

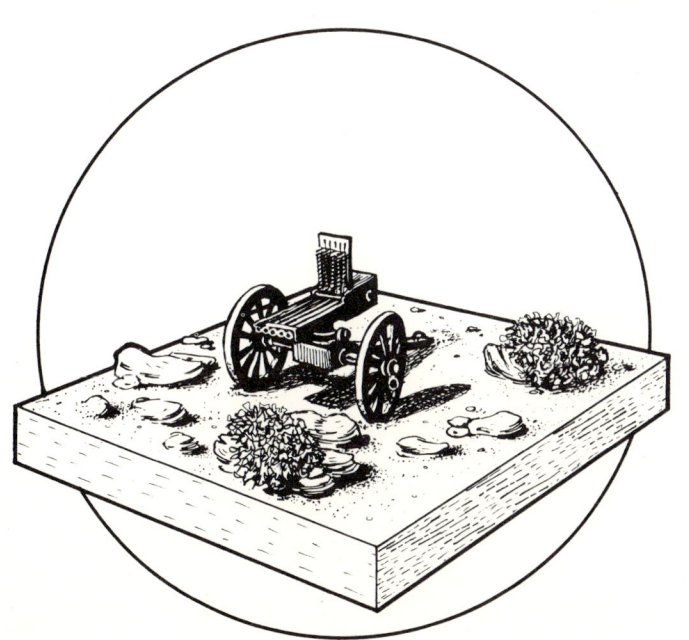
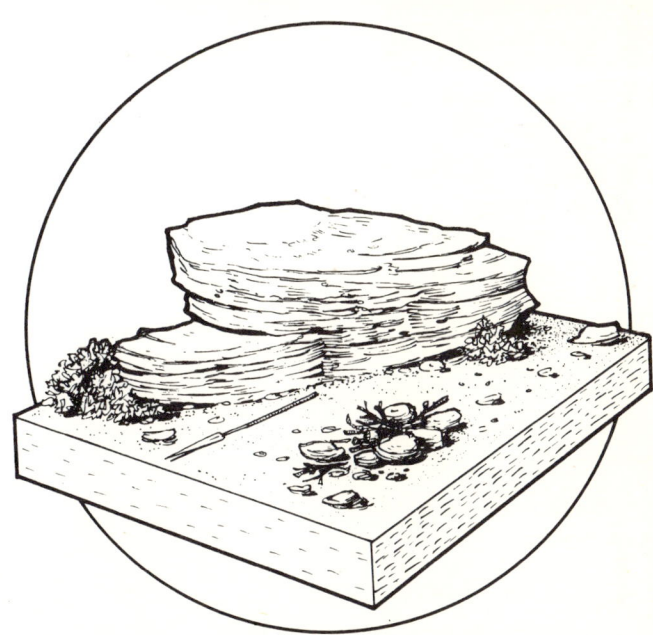

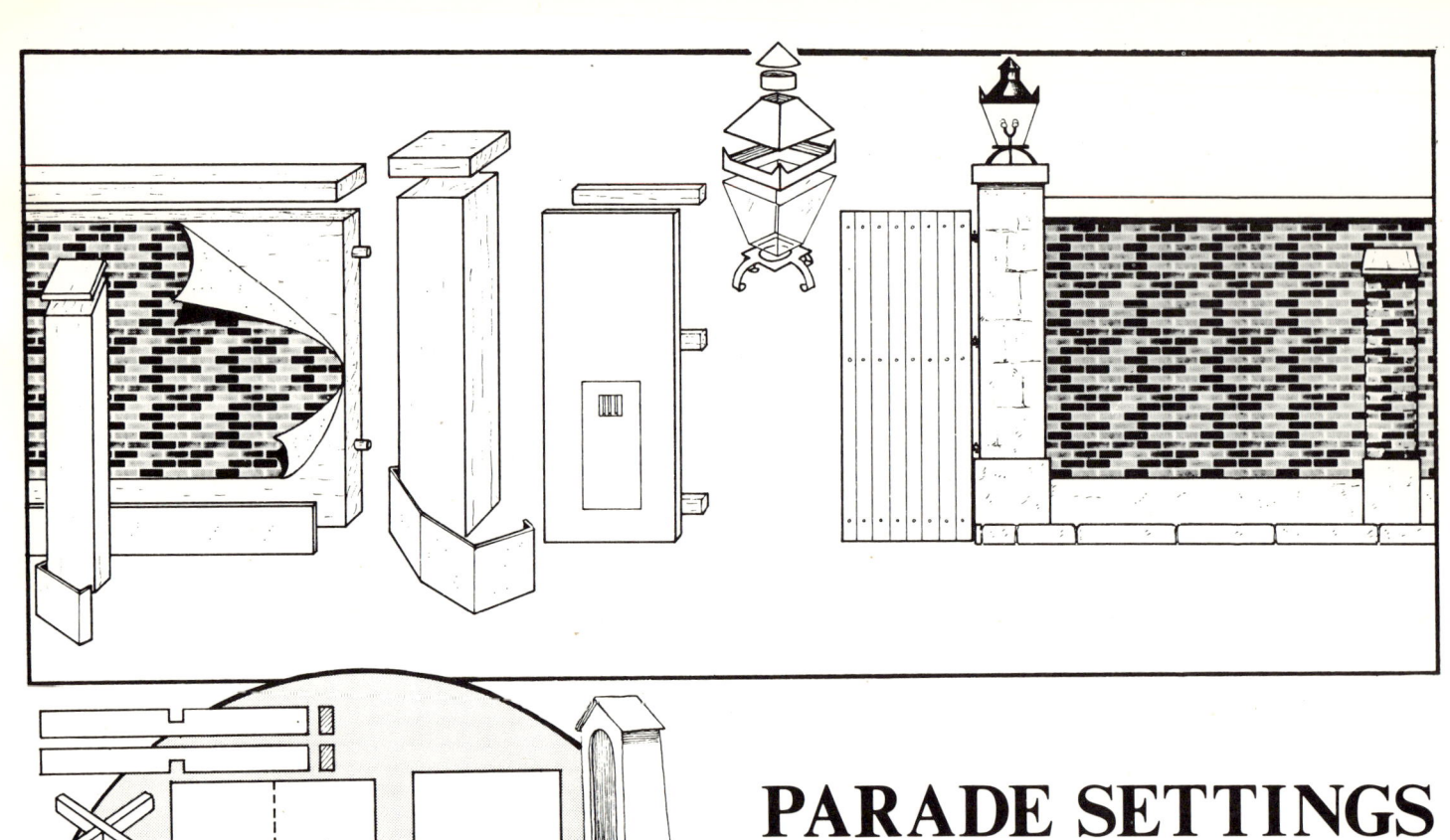

PARADE SETTINGS

The patterns made by men grouped in the precise formations of the parade ground and ceremonial activities make admirable subjects for scenic settings. These can range from simple guard mounting groups, against barrack gate or guardroom, via drill-squads and training platoons, all the way up to full scale presentations of colours or march-pasts complete with bands. Since most of such subjects will show soldiers in the formal 'drill-book' positions they are very suitable for the display of 'toy' figures, and the accent will generally be on pattern and colour, these being given added impact by the neutral gravel or asphalt parade-ground surfaces, and spartan architecture of military buildings and institutions.

Even so, considerations of good composition still apply, and the group that is thoughtfully positioned in and against its setting will have far more impact than scores of figures lined up across a base. Quite apart from accurate detail of uniform and equipment worn by the troops themselves, thought will need to be given to

the correct formations and drill-positions for that given point in a ceremony that is being represented, so here too thorough research is a necessity to avoid comic or militarily improper scenes!

There have, over the years, been a great many changes in the weapons carried on parade by soldiers, and also in the manner and style of carrying them correctly, so what is right for the period to be depicted should be clearly established in the planning stages of a parade setting; drill-books, prints or photographs will provide the answer in most cases *if they are consulted*. Military ceremonial is conducted under strict rules and procedures. Any model which claims to depict such a ceremony must get the details right, or be sure that it will attract much adverse criticism from old soldiers and others 'in the know'.

Some of the most colourful subjects for parade settings are those in which bands, corps of drums, pipes and drums, and trumpet and bugle corps are involved. Military musicians have traditionally worn distinctive uniforms, often more elaborate than those of their non-musical comrades, and just as frequently designed to provide the maximum of contrast with them. Bands adopt specific formations for marching and concert performances, with the various types of instruments taking their positions according to laid down patterns. These vary from army to army, and within armies, as do the actual instruments employed, so careful research is required to ensure an accurate representation.

Regimental standards and colours, mascots, and the more unusual sub-formations, pioneers, transport and the like, provide ideal material for fascinating parade groups.

The more glittering and glamourous side of military life can be presented in these types of formal parade groupings, giving the modeller opportunities to show uniforms, lace and accoutrements in their splendour, unsullied by dirt, grime, or the inevitable wear and tear of campaigning yet still be able to claim with truth that he met the requirements of realism!

On this page we see two distinct environment treatments by Francois Verlinden for what is virtually the same model subject, demonstrating how atmosphere or feeling of a presentation is assisted by the setting. In each case an Sdkfz 139 Marder III with its crew is depicted, but the end results differ in effect to a considerable extent. The first setting shows the crew replenishing the vehicle's ammunition supply, with a secondary subject, the vehicle commander receiving instructions via a field-telephone operator and a range-finder. Groundwork has been kept simple, but is sufficient to suggest windswept scrubby heathland with a gnarled tree. Accessories, shells and containers, a plank table, weapons and so on are used with discretion but to a good purpose. A neat touch is the helmet acting as a 'paperweight', making the scene interesting, and authentic.

A very much more tense impression is conveyed by the second diorama, in which the Marder is shown in action under the dubious protection of a ruined building. The actual placement of the model, surrounded by rubble and the debris of war, fuel and ammunition containers, is very expressive. Both settings 'tell a story', and follow the rules of good composition that are discussed elsewhere in the text. Work of this quality will undoubtedly act as an inspiration to many modellers who want to get the best out of their scenic presentations. It goes without saying that the assembly and painting of vehicles and figures in these Verlinden dioramas are absolutely first-class.

As an example of a dioramic scene, complete with groundwork, backcloth and lighting, built into a glass-fronted box, this superb presentation by one of the world's master modellers and artists must rank very high. The figure subjects, members of a patrol of French dragoons during the Peninsular campaign in the Napoleonic period, are all beautifully converted and animated from commercial kit mouldings. Into the painted plaster groundwork have been introduced roots and sprigs of lichen to represent the local vegetation, and the background painting lends distance and perspective to the scene. Displays such as this show what can be achieved by placing models in an environment which helps to establish a sense of realism.

COMBAT GROUPS

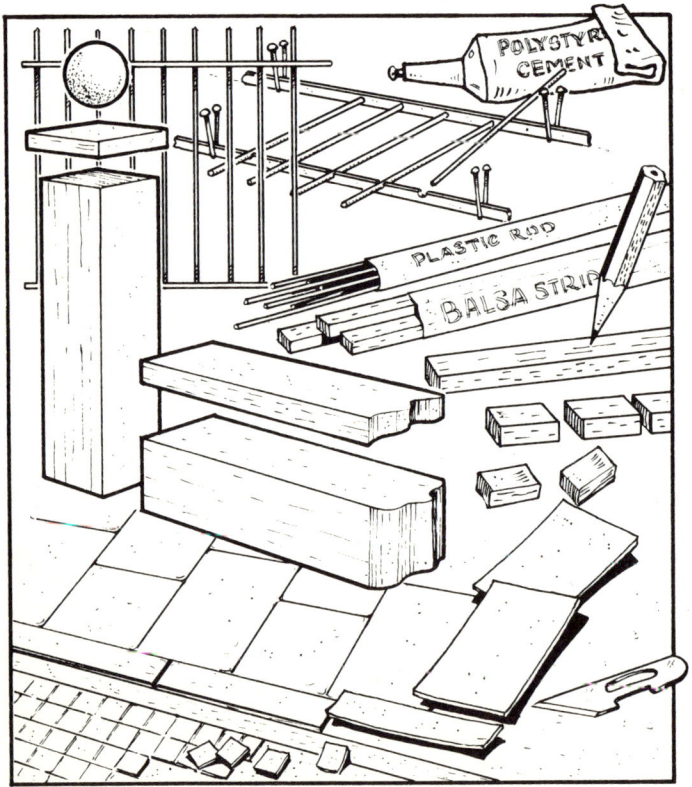

Scenes in which troops are shown in actual contact with, or close proximity to an enemy, may loosely be classified under the heading of combat groups. These are the 'in action' type presentation's and need care both in choice of subjects and their treatment, in order to make the maximum impact on the observer without becoming overly melodramatic, merely sensational or actually offensive. It is undeniable that death and destruction are inevitable concomitants of warfare, and are legitimate subjects for representation in scenes of battle if these are to be realistic, yet treatment can be restrained, even austere, and may gain greater effect by being so handled.

There is, undoubtedly, much fascination and satisfaction to be gained from the competent depiction of valorous deeds and other situations in which the calibres, physical and mental, of fighting-men are put to the test, but serious thought should be given as to what point it is desired to make, and what effect is to be achieved. This having been said, in the final analysis the choice of subject and its treatment must be left to the good taste of the individual modeller; over-emphasis of blood and thunder may well detract from the desired result.

When portraying men in combat, try so far as is possible to make their actions credible and in accordance with whatever can be established from research data referring to dress, weapons and their characteristics, and training methods of the period being represented. Remember that one of the prime purposes of military training and discipline is to so familiarise the soldier with his weapons and drills for employing them that he does the correct thing instinctively even under the stresses imposed by the sights and sounds of battle. Your trained soldier is much more likely than not to be carrying out the correct 'drills', adapted to particular circumstances maybe, but basically as taught.

Similarly, weapons have their own characteristics and effects, they are designed so, and unless it can be firmly established, (from eye-witness accounts, photographs, reliable prints or drawings and so on), that unorthodox use was made of a particular weapon on a specific occasion, it is much wiser to stick to the 'book'. For instance, avoid showing men armed with flintlock muskets delivering a volley, with each soldier, head bent, sighting along the barrel of his piece – it just wasn't done that way, and our sketches show the approved method. Animals and vehicles too have their characteristics and limitations which should be correctly portrayed.

Try also to ensure that, when a specific location is being represented rather than just a general area, i.e. the 'Ypres Salient' as opposed to 'Somewhere on the Western Front', the characteristics of soil colour, vegetation, architectural features

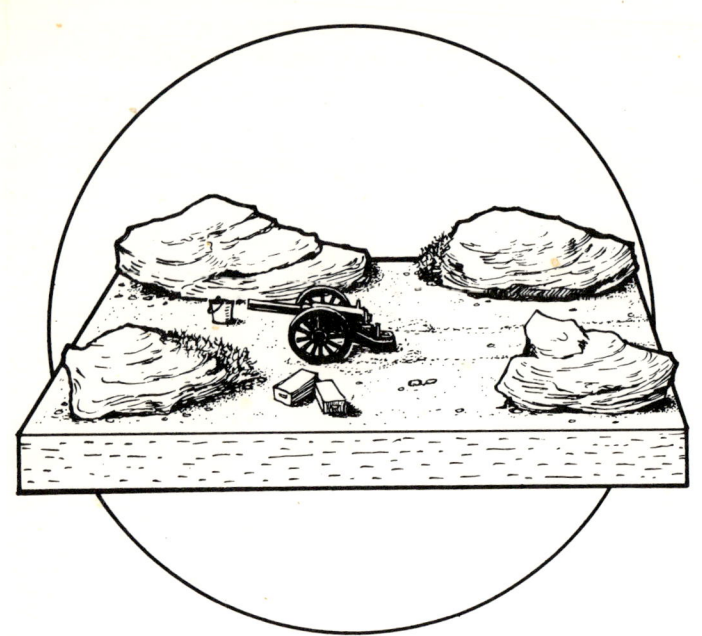

and suchlike matters in the model are consistent with what exists or existed in the real place at the time of the incident portrayed.

Make full use of the many aids, natural and manufactured, to realistic representation of scenic features; such items as railway accessory grass-matting, embossed and printed card 'stone' and 'brick' courses, cat-litter and charred veneer for rubble and fire damaged woodwork, dried grasses and mosses of various kinds to simulate larger plants, (a sprig of dried heather becomes, in scale, a large shrub or sapling!), plus of course the wide and increasing ranges of plastic moulded accessories of all kinds.

Here is an action scene set in the late-Victorian period, portraying a 2.5" mountain-gun, the 'screw-gun' immortalized in Kipling's poem, complete with its detachment of gunners and an officer. In this, as in many presentations of equipments in action, it was necessary to bear in mind the duties of each member of the detachment and his drill position in relation to the weapon, as well as to compose an interesting group. The placement of rocks and lichen frames the gun and its servants, whilst the attitude of the officer, poised above the main subject, lends a sense of urgency to the piece, which might otherwise be a little static.

The 'all-purpose' base, described on Pages 24 and 25, is here demonstrating its usefulness as a setting for the photography of a model vehicle. Extra sand has been spread over the surface, and into this can be impressed tyre-prints, ruts, etc, and if necessary the sand can be slightly dampened to provide a firmer medium for such detail. A miniature tree, in this instance a plastic item of Britains' manufacture, has been placed behind the lichen hedgerow, and the whole assembly is set up against a model railway scenic background, printed in colour on stout paper. Many variations on this basic theme can be achieved with a few bits of additional detailing, and some imagination, and it can be made to serve for models of a surprising number of periods. An 'all-purpose' base is undoubtedly a valuable component in collections where temporary display is required.

ALL PURPOSE SCENIC BASES

Of great value to collectors and providing 'instant' settings for more than one model subject, are what may conveniently be termed 'all-purpose' bases. Such backgrounds, designed to represent simple yet realistic environments, solve many problems of transportation and display, and allow the enthusiast whose prime interest is in collecting numbers of figures, vehicles or other items, to present them attractively without having each one permanently attached to its own scenic base. There are obvious advantages of simplicity, space-saving and ease of transportation in such all-purpose backgrounds, and most collectors like to have one or two at hand to cope with those pieces for which permanent settings are uncompleted or unnecessary.

It is clear that the uses for which the base is intended will have a direct bearing upon the amount and type of detail which it will incorporate. Where it is to form the background for models all representative of roughly the same period, then some feature typical of that period may well be included, but a non-specific setting will be necessary when models covering a wide time-range are to be displayed. Restraint in the use of scenic detail will serve the double purpose of allowing ample uncluttered space for models which may be of various sizes, and of permitting the grouping of the temporary occupants to be accomplished as a sound composition.

Whatever setting is decided upon, it should be constructed on a sturdy base-board, such materials as chip-board or block-board being particulary suitable as they are both robust and reasonably cheap. Plywoods and polystyrene ceiling tiles tend to be too flexible for the purpose and less likely to stand up to the rough handling that a portable stand will, undoubtedly, receive. However, ceiling tiles and polystyrene foam blocks can be bonded to the base-board and used in building up groundwork and architectural detail.

An example of an all-purpose base that has been used with great success as a background for both figures and vehicles is shown in the accompanying sketches and photographs. It has only simple detail, and consists of a wide strip of 'gravelled' surface with a narrow border of 'grass' along one side together with a lichen or moss 'hedgerow'. The textured surface is adequate to suggest a country road or the edge of a parade ground, and can be made to serve authentically for any number of situations. As an additional refinement a line of holes can be drilled along the grass verge and twigs with suitable embellishment can be inserted to make trees. Coarse sand makes good 'gravel' tamped well down over PVA adhesive, and railway accessory matting represents short grass very effectively.

SMALLER SCALES

Small scale figures up to say 30mm or just over an inch high are primarily intended for wargaming purposes, but so well-detailed are some currently available pieces that they can, when used in scenic settings, allow the modeller to produce dioramas of considerable impact. Because the reduced size of figures and background detail enables numbers of troops and large areas of ground to be represented on bases of manageable dimensions, working in small scale is especially suitable for the portrayal of complete parade or combat scenes, where the observer's eye can take in the whole panorama of an occasion or incident without difficulty. Buildings, whether undamaged or ruined can be presented in their entirety, as can trees, bridges and architectural structures that would require a very great deal of space if carried out in 'standard' scale or larger, and there is little problem involved in portraying even small villages and field works to their full extent.

Since most of the smaller figure scales are identical with or similar to several popular railway modelling scales, much of the enormous variety of railway scenic accessory material can be employed in the production of military settings, and used in conjunction with the almost equally numerous ranges of wargaming items, will permit a strong air of realism to be achieved in almost any background.

'Natural' materials can also be extremely effective. Moss or lichen on fine twigs makes really convincing trees, or used on its own represents shrubs and hedges with fidelity. Sand serves for coarse gravel, shingle, ploughed or churned up earth when painted appropriately, and many tiny garden or hedgerow plants can be made to stand in for scrub and woodland with great success. Rocky crags and cliff-faces can be simulated excellently well with strips of cork bark, obtainable in most model shops or florists, whilst boulders and scree need no more than the intelligent use of pebbles and rock chippings from garden or sea-shore.

Several manufacturers of small scale figures, vehicles and

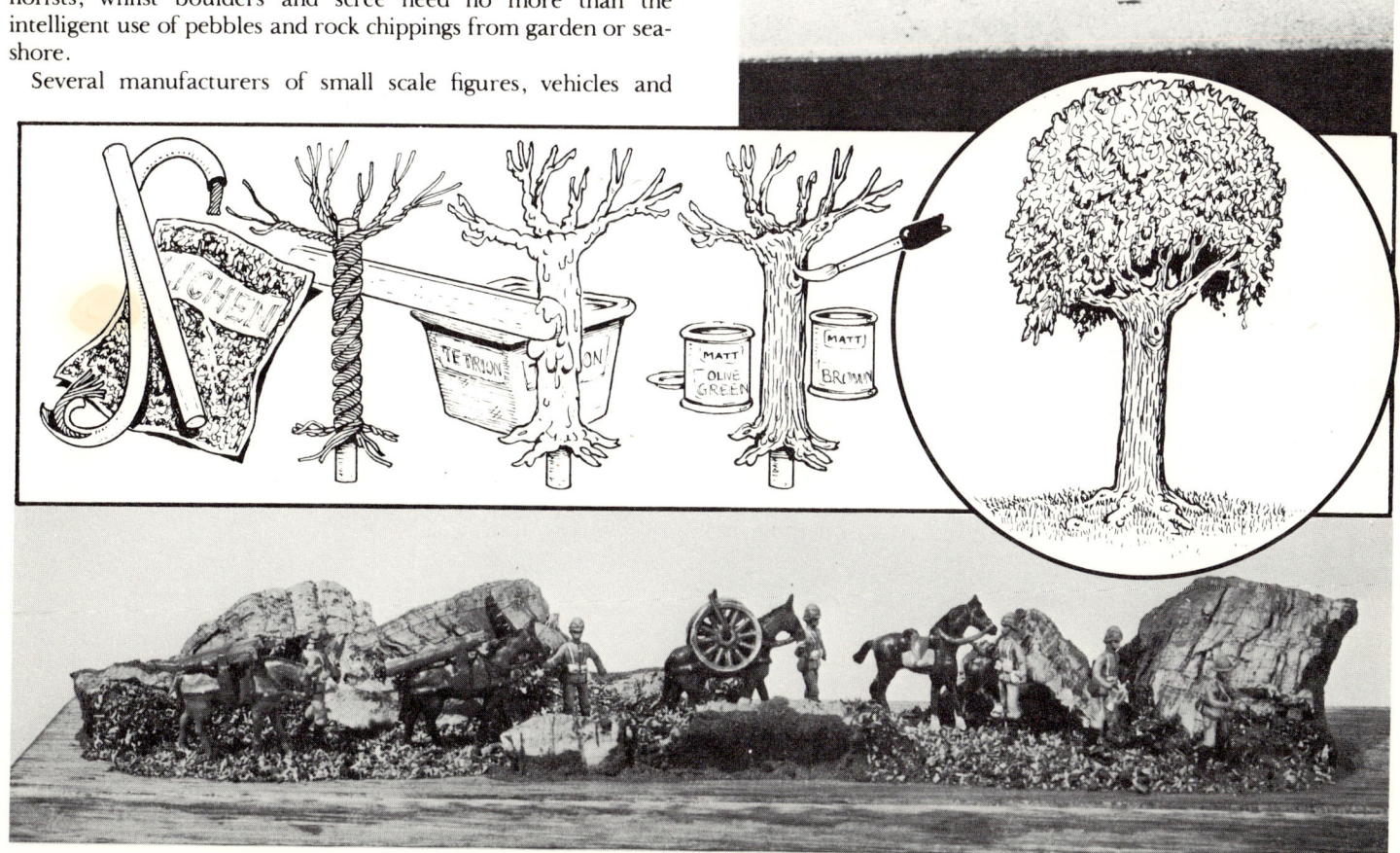

equipment put plastic kits of scenic features, field works, military installations and all kinds of accessories at reasonable cost, so, all in all, the needs of the modeller in these scales are very well catered for.

It should be borne in mind that the rules of good composition

apply to scenic work in these as in larger scales, whilst the necessity to guard against clutter in the presentation may be even greater.

SPECIALISED SETTINGS

Certain types of terrain may be said to be 'specialized', and their representation needs extra care if convincing results are to be achieved. Some examples of such terrain would be: desert, jungle, water (rivers, ponds and the like), and snowscapes. All can be depicted successfully, and no modeller need be deterred from attempting to convey their particular characteristics.

Desert

This can vary from the flowing 'sea of sand' to rock and scrub covered wastelands. In most desert regions gravel and rock are at least as plentiful as sand, and are in fact more likely to support military activity so difficult is it to get about in deep, soft sand. Holiday trips to the sea-shore and visits to the local builders'-yard will yield a surprising variety of sand consistencies from almost

dust to near gravel. A wide selection of sand types, with fine gravel and rock chippings will provide the basis for all sorts of desert surfaces in many scales. All can be applied, after the underlying form of the ground has been established, by being sprinkled densely over a thick coating of PVA adhesive, tamped gently in with a spatula or similar instrument, and then carefully shaken to remove excess material. Alternatively the sand can be mixed with flour and water paste, spread over the ground contours and allowed to dry. Rocks, tyre and track impressions, scrub and camel-thorn can be pressed into the mixture in both methods before the adhesive has set, plants being simulated with dried lichens or moss. A final application overall of powdered pastels in sandy shades will produce a good effect of dust on the completed scene.

Jungle

Perhaps the most difficult of all types of terrain to reproduce, it can be made quite convincingly with the aid of various 'natural' items. Certain grasses with fine seedheads, dried, dyed green and secured in bunches make excellent 'bamboo'. Small rock-plants, cacti, succulents and even heathers represent jungle undergrowth and foliage very well, whilst the ever-useful sphagnum mosses

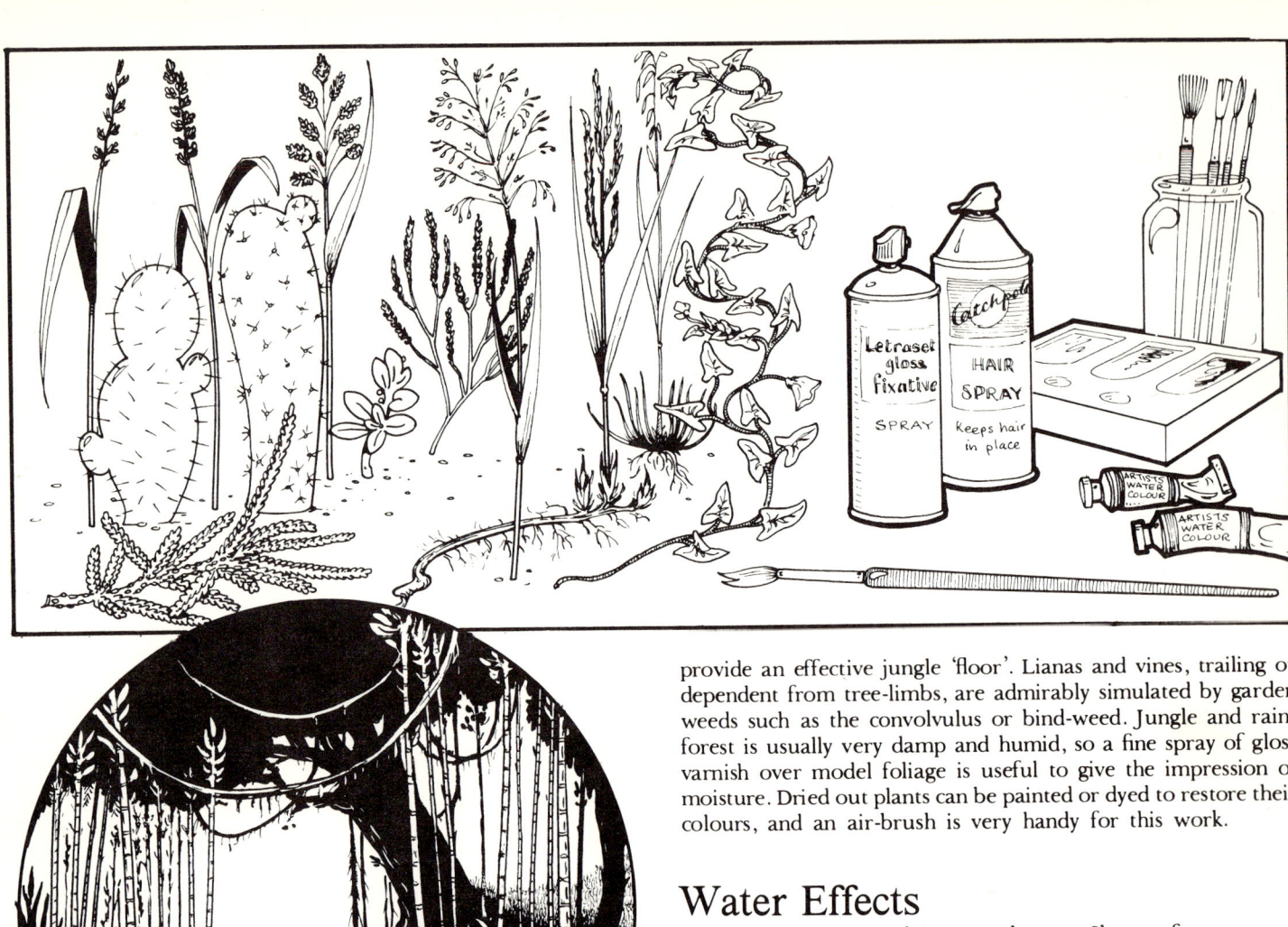

provide an effective jungle 'floor'. Lianas and vines, trailing or dependent from tree-limbs, are admirably simulated by garden weeds such as the convolvulus or bind-weed. Jungle and rain-forest is usually very damp and humid, so a fine spray of gloss varnish over model foliage is useful to give the impression of moisture. Dried out plants can be painted or dyed to restore their colours, and an air-brush is very handy for this work.

Water Effects

These can be achieved in several ways. Sheets of transparent plastic or glass over hollowed-out areas suitably painted and strewn with gravel and weeds convey the appearance of clear, still water. Crumpled cellophane, touched here and there with white paint to represent foam, serves for fast running water, rapids and so on, and rippled glass can have a similar effect. Really deep water, lakes and the sea, are simulated well with plaster of Paris worked before setting into waves, breakers or other patterns, then painted and repeatedly varnished to give a highly glossed surface. Clear-cast resins make good still water, and can be self-coloured or used clear over painted 'beds' as for sheet glass and plastic, remembering that not all materials and paints are

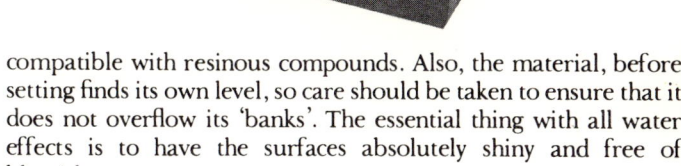

compatible with resinous compounds. Also, the material, before setting finds its own level, so care should be taken to ensure that it does not overflow its 'banks'. The essential thing with all water effects is to have the surfaces absolutely shiny and free of blemishes.

Snow

In most instances a skim of plaster of Paris over scenic contours is satisfactory for snow effects, the plaster, when dry, being over-painted with matt white paint mixed with talcum powder to give a more realistic surface. A mixture of salt and alum spread over white PVA glue is also effective, particularly where snow is shown lying along the branches of trees, on the tops of walls, or on window-sills, etc.

Field-Engineering

This term includes such settings as trenches, redoubts, redans, block-houses, and temporarily fortified positions of all kinds. Earthworks, sand-bags, corrugated-iron and barbed wire are the principal materials, with wooden planks, logs, trench-board and so on as accessories. The sand and flour-paste mixture described under the 'Desert' heading, when painted in earth colours serves well for shell-torn ground, strips of veneer make good boards and planks, cut lengths of straight twigs duplicate logs, and twisted fuse-wire with extra barbs bound on at intervals depicts barbed-wire with effect. Treat water-logged shell-holes, etc as for small ponds or pools.

PURPOSE-BUILT FORTIFICATIONS

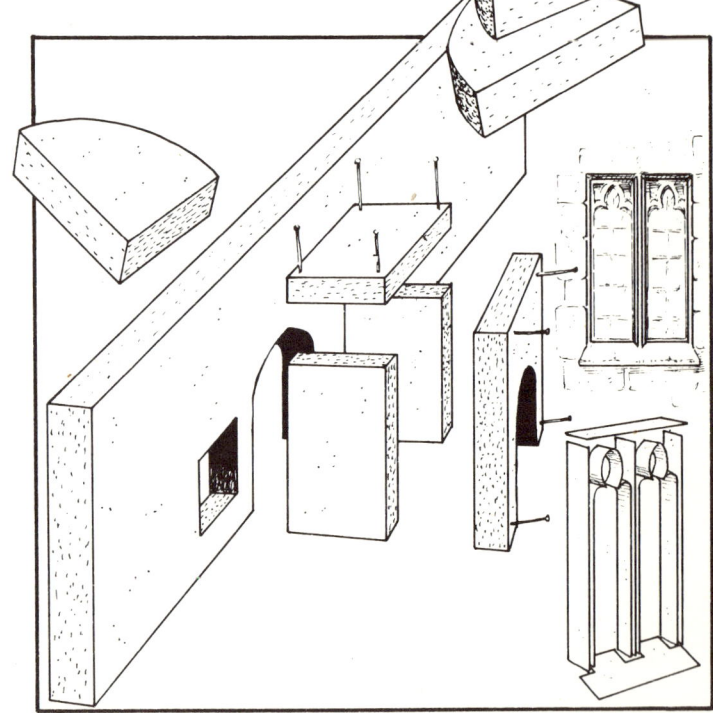

By this term is meant the whole range of permanent stoutly-built works such as castles, forts and defensive-lines that constitute military fortifications outside the range of field-engineering. They make excellent settings for the display of models of mediaeval subjects, 18th and 19th century garrison troops with their guns and equipment, and of course, present day ceremonial and pageantry. There are many real-life specimens of such works dotted about all over the world, most in ruins nowadays, but a fair number, the Tower of London, Dover Castle, and fortifications in the Mediterranean to name but a few, which survive as complete examples, down to the last floor-board, and plenty of books and pamphlets covering them in detail with plans and drawings included. Most British Castles in the care of the Department of the Environment have these inexpensive publications available to visitors. These mostly cover mediaeval buildings, but many Roman antiquities, like Hadrians Wall, have similar coverage, so obtaining reference data from which to construct models of fortifications should not prove to be too difficult.

Since most military fortifications of a permanent nature were built in stone, different periods having characteristic methods of laying the courses, (and arch door and window shapes), the main problem in modelling them is to achieve a convincing effect of stone. This can be achieved by actually carving courses into plaster applied over formers, and can be seen in the superlative work of Major Bob Rowe at Woburn.

Expanded Polystyrene blocks and tiles can also be carved and impressed to show stone coursing and if a very thin layer of plaster is spread over the polystyrene and etched before fully dry, most excellent effects can be obtained.

Another very satisfactory source of model 'stonework' is the wealth of printed and embossed card stocks produced principally with railway modelling in mind. These are available in various scales, and can very easily be cut out and glued on to cardboard, wood or expanded polystyrene formers to give an extremely realistic effect. However, most printed surfaces have a slight sheen on them so a coat of matt spray, such a Letraset Matt is advisable for the best results. Railway grass matting is useful for the swards associated with castles and forts, and very thin strips of the same material applied along the bases of walls at ground level gives a convincing impression of the weeds that are sometimes found in these locations in real life.

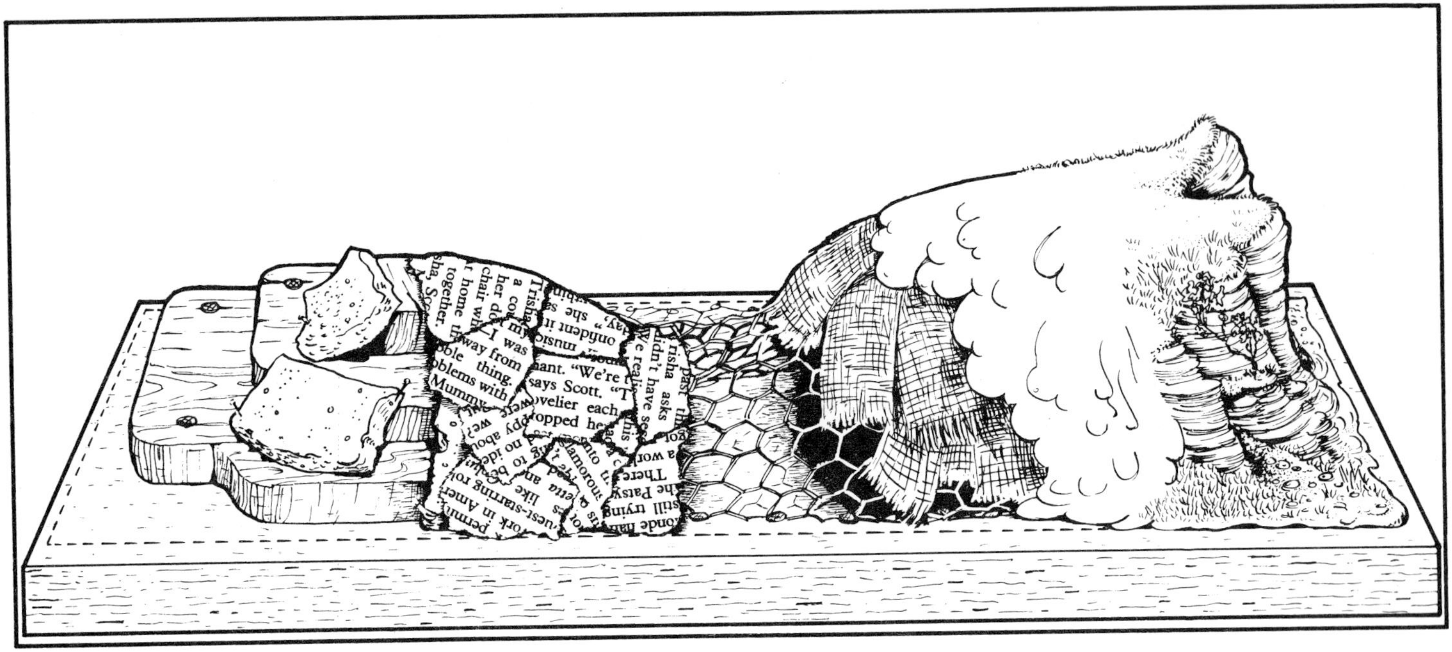

Modelling fortifications is, in effect, building in miniature and requires attention to such matters as plumb-lines, pitches, correct placement of angles, buttresses, stairways, etc., and the relevant styles of architecture for the period in which the building to be represented was constructed.

BASES

In the foregoing pages were described a number of scenic settings, from very simple to relatively complex; let us now look again at actual physical make up, since the conception and composition of presentations need to be supported by satisfactory practical interpretations.

The foundations for settings must be absolutely solid if difficulties in the fixing of groundwork, models, and accessory detail, and in transportation of the piece are to be avoided.

Materials from which firm, robust bases can be made vary in price and availability, but some of the more common and acceptably priced are blockboard, chipboard and fibreboard, all of which, in reasonable thicknesses and areas, will maintain a flat, warp-free surface. Fibreboard in the form of cake-stands, can also be obtained in various pre-cut shapes, but is more expensive.

Some multi-ply sheet woods, and floor or shelving boards are suitable for model bases, provided they are resistant to warping.

In most cases, decorative veneers applied to the edges, and sheets of baize, felt or flock-paper to the undersides of bases will give them a more professional finish.

Purpose-made bases can also be obtained from many model shops, and these are usually complete ready for the addition of models and setting.

GROUND-WORK

A satisfactorily solid base having been constructed, it is then possible to build-up the 'ground-work' of the setting, that is the contours and textures of the environment. Flat ground can be applied as a thin coating of plaster or self-hardening modelling-clay, into which foot and hoof prints, tyre marks, ruts, shell-holes, etc., can be impressed whilst the material is still malleable. Some modellers use Plasticine for ground-work, and this is excellent but will always be more or less malleable, and should not be handled once the contours have been established.

Textures, such as grass, gravel, soil, stone and so on, are achieved with appropriately coloured sands, flock powders, rock chips, rope or sizal strands and model railway 'matting', pressed into or sprinkled on to the surface.

For mounds, slopes, river beds and uneven ground generally, the contours can be built up with formers overlaid with paper strips glued on, netting, or plaster-bandages, providing a firm crust for the final texturing. Plaster should be self-coloured with dyes or paints at the mixing stage to avoid glaring white areas if it subsequently becomes chipped. Similarly, exposed edges of ground-work look better if painted black or earth colour.

SCENIC DETAIL

Into the ground-work can be added such items of vegetation and architecture as are necessary to complete the environment for the model subjects.

Lichens, mosses, tiny plants, grasses and dyed tea-leaves become hedges, shrubs, scrub and foliage of various kinds, with twigs, heather shoots and seedling roots providing the trunks and limbs for saplings and trees.

Lengths of fibre from unravelled sizal or hempen string, hairs from old paint, paste or shaving brushes, and fine dried real grass will act as clumps of coarse grass, corn, reeds and rushes, with grains of sand glued on to make seed heads. Small pieces of dyed coconut matting also simulate tall grass or corn fields.

Stone walls can be built with tiny rock fragments, or represented by carving stone courses into plaster applied over formers. The same methods are suitable for brickwork, walls of buildings, etc., the underlying shapes of which can be cut out of plywood, fibre-board or expanded polystyrene sheet.

Into the simulation of woodwork, floorboards, planks and so on can be pressed strips of veneer, matchsticks and balsa or beech strip wood.

Water is represented by glass, resin, painted varnish, cellophane or clear acetate sheet, which also serves well for window panes and other glasswork.

There is also the enormous wealth of purpose made accessories, covering almost every requirement.

Plan the settings well, carry them out carefully, and your models will indeed mirror life.

ACKNOWLEDGEMENTS

The Authors gratefully acknowledge the help and co-operation of the following, for the provision of models and facilities in connection with the preparation of this book:

Lyn Sangster
Keith and Teresa Lister
Bob Denness
Dennis Green
Graham Brown
Jim Booth
John Cuiffo
Bill Berry
Ray Newbury
F. Verlinden
Anthony Dilley
E. Leliepvre